CELEBRATING THE FAMILY NAME OF WU

Celebrating the Family Name of Wu

Walter the Educator

Silent King Books
a WhichHead Entertainment Imprint

Copyright © 2024 by Walter the Educator

All rights reserved. No part of this book may be reproduced in any manner whatsoever without written permission except in the case of brief quotations embodied in critical articles and reviews.

First Printing, 2024

Disclaimer

This book is a literary work; the story is not about specific persons, locations, situations, and/or circumstances unless mentioned in a historical context. Any resemblance to real persons, locations, situations, and/or circumstances is coincidental. This book is for entertainment and informational purposes only. The author and publisher offer this information without warranties expressed or implied. No matter the grounds, neither the author nor the publisher will be accountable for any losses, injuries, or other damages caused by the reader's use of this book. The use of this book acknowledges an understanding and acceptance of this disclaimer.

Celebrating the Family Name of Wu is a memory book that belongs to the Celebrating Family Name Book Series by Walter the Educator. Collect them all and more books at WaltertheEducator.com

USE THE EXTRA SPACE TO DOCUMENT YOUR FAMILY MEMORIES THROUGHOUT THE YEARS

WU

Beneath the heavens, vast and blue,

There shines the steadfast name of Wu.

A lineage rich, both deep and wide,

With honor strong and hearts as guide.

From mountains tall to rivers grand,

The Wu name shapes the ancient land.

Through changing winds and shifting tide,

The Wu endure, their strength their pride.

In scholars' scrolls and poets' rhymes,

The Wu have stood the test of time.

A name of wisdom, calm yet bold,

Their story written in lines of gold.

Builders of dreams, defenders of peace,

The Wu name grows, it will not cease.

With every dawn, their light takes flight,

A beacon clear through day and night.

From ink-stained hands to warriors' steel,

The Wu name holds a noble seal.

A family strong, with roots profound,

A voice of unity resounds.

Through storms of life, they face with grace,

The Wu name carves its timeless place.

Each generation stands anew,

Carrying forth what's just and true.

In verdant fields and bustling streets,

The Wu name whispers, the world it greets.

A tale of love, of hope, of care,

A bond unbroken, beyond compare.

Through history's scroll, their light persists,

The Wu name etched in ancient lists.

Their spirit flows like rivers wide,

A current fierce, yet dignified.

With hearts of fire and minds of stone,

The Wu stand tall, their legacy grown.

A family bound by honor's thread,

A legacy bright, forever spread.

So sing of Wu, in joy and pride,

A name that stands through time and tide.

Forever shining, steadfast and true,

A lasting symbol, the name of Wu.

ABOUT THE CREATOR

Walter the Educator is one of the pseudonyms for Walter Anderson. Formally educated in Chemistry, Business, and Education, he is an educator, an author, a diverse entrepreneur, and he is the son of a disabled war veteran. "Walter the Educator" shares his time between educating and creating. He holds interests and owns several creative projects that entertain, enlighten, enhance, and educate, hoping to inspire and motivate you. Follow, find new works, and stay up to date with Walter the Educator™

at WaltertheEducator.com

www.ingramcontent.com/pod-product-compliance
Lightning Source LLC
LaVergne TN
LVHW052009060526
838201LV00059B/3929